Finding Your Equine Soul Mate: A Guide to Buying Your First Horse

Michele Cook

ISBN: 1541194063
ISBN-13: 978-1541194069

DEDICATION

To my husband, for putting up with such a horse crazy girl, and all of her horse crazy friends.

To my children, Brandon, Amanda, Carl J and Katie, never stop dreaming.

CONTENTS

ACKNOWLEDGMENTS

This book would not be possible without all of the horses I have ridden and the owners who allowed me to ride them. Special thanks goes out to my former students and clients. Thank you for trusting me with your children, both human and equine.

I also have to thank the Chronicle of the Horse community for donating many of the stories you see in this book. Thank you for your support in my endeavors.

I would also like to thank my editor, Hannah Bauman for putting up with my sometimes grouchy responses to her edits.

To my beta readers Audra Coats-Hudson and Julie Hage thank you for reading and critiquing this book, you have made it so much better.

To Charleen Nicholson, thank you for your help with the cover art, I may be bald right now if it wasn't for your help.

Finally, to Rachel Russell, thank you for your help in formatting this book and answering all of my publishing questions. You were truly a life saver.

INTRODUCTION

I have been involved in horses from the time I was a white haired little girl begging for a pony for Christmas. Since then, I have learned a lot about the relationship between horse and human. In my four decades on this planet I have learned that finding your equine soul mate is much like finding your human one. Except horses don't leave the seat up, nag you about your dirty laundry or come with a mother-in-law.

Horses are big, expensive animals. The right one can bring you joy and confidence and the wrong one can bring you frustration, exhaustion, and even injury. Finding your equine soul mate will take time and effort, but it will be worth it in the end. Your equine soul mate should complement your personality. You are looking for a horse you can learn to trust. You want your horse to be a willing partner with a kind disposition.

Just like in finding your human soul mate, personality trumps looks every time. No matter how pretty a horse may be, if he doesn't have the right attitude, it is a recipe for disaster. I have ridden hundreds of horses in my career - some for five minutes, some for five years - but in each case, the personality of the horse was what made me fall in love with them.

I have seen people who are on horses with too much energy, not enough energy, mismatched personalities between horse and rider, and horses forced into disciplines they aren't suited for. The people riding these horses did not look like they were having fun. There were some who were struggling to get an unsuitable horse over a jump. Some were clinging to the back of a horse that had too much energy for their skill level. A lot of tears were shed, some in frustration, some in fear, and some in pain.

On the flip side, I have seen horses and riders so perfectly matched, it was a thing of beauty to watch them interact. The horse seemed to know what the rider was thinking at every turn. When horse or rider did make a mistake, the other partner picked up the slack and everyone came home safe. Finding a partnership like this is what makes riding horses fun. It takes away the fear and worry of sitting atop a thousand pound animal and replaces it with exhilaration and trust.

Throughout this book you will find some personal stories about horse shopping. Some are humorous, some describe the frustration of horse shopping and some are a little scary. All of these stories are true. I included them to give you a bit of perspective. You might run into similar situations or perhaps something even stranger. If you do, feel free write it down and send it in so I can include it in my next book.

I want to thank all of the people who submitted these stories for taking a minute and writing them down and then graciously giving me permission to use them in this book.

CHAPTER 1
GETTING STARTED

The first few sections of this book will prepare you for your search to find the perfect horse. Some readers may already know the discipline they want to ride in and some may already have an equine pro or trainer. Either way, it is a good idea to read through these sections to give yourself a good reminder on what it takes to find your equine soul mate.

Knowing what it takes to be successful in your chosen discipline and understanding your skill level in that discipline will dictate the type of horse you should be looking for.

Having an equine pro to help you in your search will give you a good idea on where your skill level is and what is required in your discipline. It will also give you more contacts to find your dream horse and a set of well-educated eyes that will see things about a prospective horse you might miss.

Disciplines

Horses are versatile creatures that have been utilized for various pursuits throughout history. They have been beasts of burden plowing the fields, sleek racing machines, and sporting companions for many a leisure rider

Before you invest any money in your equine partner, you need to decide what discipline interests you the most. Do you want to soar over jumps? Take a ride through the woods on a summer evening? Maybe you are interested in showing your four legged friend off as he pulls your carriage down the road.

Knowing what you want to do with your horse before you buy him will go a long way towards creating a lasting partnership. Just like humans, certain horses are built to excel at certain things. Can you imagine Shaq as a gymnast? Many disciplines do not have a specific breed requirement to participate , but there are general build and body types that will perform some disciplines better than others.

The following is a list of disciplines with a brief description of each one. Keep in mind this is not a complete list of disciplines; this is just a list of the most popular pursuits. If you find a discipline you are particularly interested in, there are additional references and book recommendations at the end of each section. You can use them to find out more about what the discipline requires and the training techniques used in each discipline.

Barrel Racing

Barrel racing is a speed event. The object of the sport is to race around three barrels in a clover leaf pattern, with the fastest horse and rider combination winning the day. Knocking over a barrel will get you a time penalty, so competitors must take care when galloping to each barrel.

Barrel racing is a fun sport that has levels for the younger and more green riders to the advanced riders you see on the professional rodeo circuit. The horses used for this sport are typically smaller, more compact horses that can turn quickly and get moving fast. Quarter Horses and Quarter Horse crosses are a popular choice, but there is no breed requirement for most contests. If the horse is fast and can turn on a dime, he will do well as a barrel racer.

Resources

National Barrel Horse Association - https://www.nbha.com/

Women's Professional Rodeo Association - http://www.wpra.com/

Books

Charmayne James on Barrel Racing – Charmayne James

Barrel Racing for Fun and Fast Times – Sharon Camirillo

Dressage

Dressage is the art of training a horse. Dressage is like a dance between horse and rider and when done correctly, it is beautiful to watch. In a dressage competition, the horse and rider perform a preset pattern called a test. Each test is judged on the horse's quality of gaits, willingness to obey it's rider, straightness , and suppleness, as well as the rider's seat and effectiveness. Each movement is given a score and the scores are tallied at the end. The scores are announced as the percentage completed of the total possible score. Unlike math class, a 70% in dressage is more than passing; it is considered a strong score.

Dressage competitions are progressive. They

begin with tests that only require walking and trotting, called intro level tests, and competitions go all the way up to the Grand Prix level. This gives any level of horse and rider the opportunity to show in a dressage competition.

All horses should know the basics of dressage and there is no breed requirement for showing in dressage. At the lower levels, many different breeds have been successful. A horse with good gaits and a good mind will be more important than breed at the lower levels. On the other hand, you will see almost exclusively warmbloods at the higher levels of competition. Hanoverians, Dutch Warmbloods, Swedish Warmbloods, and Trakehners are all popular in the upper levels of dressage.

Resources

United States Dressage Federation - http://www.usdf.org/

Books

Complete Training of Horse and Rider in the Principles of Classical Horsemanship – Alex Podhajsky

Dressage in Harmony: From Basic to Grand Prix – Walter A. Zettl

What is A Warmblood?

Warmbloods are a designation of a group of breeds that originated in Europe in the 1700 and 1800s. The breeds were developed as carriage horses and war horses. People were looking for horses that could carry a soldier in full armor and pull a heavy decorative carriage. They wanted the horses to be able to do these things and have the speed and agility of a lighter horse. So larger draft breeds were crossed with Arabian and Thoroughbreds and then refined through consistent breeding standards. The breeds are usually named after the region they were developed in; for example the Hanoverian was developed in the Hanover region of Germany and the Selle Francis was developed in France.

Driving

Driving is a timeless activity, and humans have been using horses for driving for centuries. From the time of the Romans, horses have been used to pull some type of apparatus. Farmers used horses to pull a plow, kings were pulled in golden carriages and warriors fought battles from chariots. While driving is an equestrian sport, you can also drive for leisure. Whether it's a "one horsed open sleigh" in the winter, a carriage through New York City, or just going for a drive through the country, driving is both a hobby and a sport.

Driving is an incredibly diverse sport; you have everything from 12 Budweiser Clydesdales hitched to a large wagon to a tiny 26 inch tall miniature horse pulling a small cart. Any horse can be driven, and there are many different competitions for different types of driving horses. This discipline is really up to your imagination. Find a good equine pro in your area to help you train your horse for driving.

Resources

The American Driving Society - http://americandrivingsociety.org/

The United States Equestrian Federation (Combined Driving Division) - https://www.usef.org/_iframes/breedsdisciplines/discipline/alldriving.aspx

Books

Driving a Harness Horse: A Step-By-Step Guide - Sallie Walrond

Driving Horses: How to Harness, Align, and Hitch your Horse for Work or Play - Steve Bowers

3 Day Eventing

Three day eventing (or eventing for short) is a sport known as the triathlon of horse sports. On the first day, horses and riders compete in a dressage competition. On the second day, a cross country competition takes place, where horse and rider gallop across country, jumping solid obstacles as they go. On the third day, horses and riders compete in a traditional show jumping competition.

Training for three day eventing includes all three disciplines. Many times , riders will have a main trainer who understands the ins and outs of three day eventing, but riders will also train with other pros who are specialists in dressage or show jumping. This sport is like three competitions rolled into one and it takes great skill and stamina to compete successfully.

Any horse that has the stamina and jumping ability can compete in eventing. The great Teddy O'Connor was just under 14.2 hands and competed at the highest level of the sport. In the upper echelon, most horses are Thoroughbreds or Thoroughbred crosses. These horses usually have the stamina, athletic ability, and speed required for a high level eventing horse. However, if you're just starting out, a horse that is willing and sound is most important.

Resources

United States Eventing Association - http://www.useventing.com/

Books

Modern Eventing with Phillip Dutton: The Complete Resource: Training, Conditioning, and

Competing in All Three Phases – Phillip Dutton and Boyd Martin

101 Eventing Tips: Essentials For Combined Training And Horse Trials (101 Tips) – James Wofford

Hunters

A hunter is a horse that competes in hunter classes. A hunter class is a jumping class held over eight to ten jumps. At the lowest level, those jumps may be tiny cross rails and at the highest level, they may be four -foot-high jumps with a four-foot-wide spread to match.

This class is judged on a horse's ability to jump well, with knees up and even and a rounded back (called bascule). The horse is also judged on consistent pace, temperament, and the overall picture the horse presents to the judge.

There is no breed requirement to compete in a hunter class. Any horse that can jump in good form and show a consistent pace can do well in a hunter class. Like many other horse sports, many breeds do well at the lower levels. At the upper levels, warmblood breeds like Hanoverians, Dutch Warmbloods and Trakehners dominate the standings.

Resources

United States Hunter Jumper Association - https://www.ushja.org/

Books

Hunter Seat Equitation – George H. Morris

Learning to Ride, Hunt and Show – Gordon Wright

Reining

Reining is a pattern sport performed in a western saddle. In reining, you are showing off how well a horse responds to your aides and how much control you have with a small movement of the reins. In fact, most reining horses are trained to respond to weight and leg cues more than reins. The reins are left long and loopy to show how easily the horse is controlled.

This sport is fast paced, requiring sliding stops, fast spins, and quick rollbacks. There are levels available for beginners to advanced riders, but there is one thing to make note of: unless you are showing as a professional, you must own the horse you are showing. This is true even at the lowest levels. The National Reining Horse Association is working on making the entry level of the sport a little bit easier for newcomers, but as of this writing, you must own the horse to show in this discipline.

Reining horses do not have to be a particular breed, but small, compact horses are known to excel in this discipline. Breeds like the American Paint Horse, the Quarter Horse, and the Appaloosa might fall into this category.

Resources

The National Reining Horse Association - http://nrha1.com/

Books

How to Train the Reining Horse – Tom McCann

Reining Essentials: How to excel in Western's Hottest Sport – Sandy Collier and Jennifer Forsberg Meyer

Show Jumping

Show jumping is a speed event in which you jump a course of fences faster than your other competitors without knocking any fences down. This is one of the most popular horse sports in the world because it is so much fun for riders and spectators alike.

In the first round, riders are given a course of jumps to complete and a time allowed for completion. After the first round, any horse and rider combinations that went clear (all of the fences were left up and the pair was faster than the time allowed) will compete in a jump off. The jump off is fast and furious. The riders are given a shortened course to ride and must jump the course as fast as they can while leaving the jumps up. The rider with the fastest time and the fewest fences down will win the day.

Show jumping is open to any breed of horse. Most horses are warmbloods or Thoroughbreds but there are always exceptions in show jumping. This includes a 14.1h pony named Stroller, the only pony to compete in the Olympics. At the lower levels of this discipline, almost every breed of horse has competed and won prizes. If you plan on competing in show jumping, a willing mount with a good jumping style is a bigger component than breed.

Resources

United States Hunter Jumper Association - https://www.ushja.org/

Books

Anne Kursinski's Riding and Jumping Clinic – Anne Kursinski

Peter Leone's Show Jumping Clinic – Peter Leone

Trail Riding

Trail riding is enjoyed by most equine enthusiasts. Some use it to give a horse a break from the daily rigors of training, some compete in competitive trail riding, and some just enjoy being out on the trail.

A mistake I often hear about trail riding is "oh you just trail ride." While many people think you simply sit on the horse and do nothing, trail riding requires good control of your horse. As a rider, you must learn to balance yourself and your horse on uneven terrain, go up and down different grades, cross water, and know how to handle wild animals spooking your horse. There is certainly more to trail riding then just sitting on the horse.

If you are interested in competing in trail riding, there are competitive trail rides where you will be asked to complete a set of obstacles at a specific gait. You may be asked to drag a log at a trot, cross a stream at a walk, or jump a small log. These are all obstacles you might face out on the trail.

There is no breed restriction for trail riding, and any horse can be a good trail horse. If you are looking for a trail horse, you want to find a horse with good feet that has comfortable gaits and a quiet mind.

Resources

North American Trail Ride Conference - http://www.natrc.org/

Books

Goodnight's Guide to Great Trail Riding – Julie Goodnight

Trail Riding: Trail, Prepare, Pack Up and Hit the Trail – Rhonda Massingham Hart

He Was This High

I called on a pony that was for sale. On the telephone, I asked the seller, "how tall is your pony." The guy on the other end of the line said, "Well, he comes up to about here on me."

This of course did me no good as I couldn't see through the telephone line!

Esther, Maine

CHAPTER 2
FINDING YOUR EQUINE PRO OR TRAINER

Before beginning your search for your equine soul mate, you should take some lessons in your chosen discipline. Every top rated equestrian has a trainer to help them, so there is no shame in taking some lessons before you purchase your new horse. This is doubly true if you are riding in a new discipline and even more important if you have never ridden before.

To get you started, contact the national group associated with your discipline. They may have a list of qualified instructors and if not, they will be able to guide you to local groups that can help you find an instructor in your area. After you get a few names together, you'll need to investigate the quality of those trainers.

Horses and all things associated with them are "buyer beware" situations , so it's wise to do your homework before you sign up for a long block of lessons with a particular trainer. Starting with the national association can help, but it is no guarantee of the quality of the recommended pro.

In the US, there is no standardized test or license for horse trainers(with the exception of Massachusetts, which requires a state license to be a riding instructor). You must do your own research. You can use message boards or a local Facebook groups to get a general feeling about the equine pro you are interested in working with, and even Google can be a big help in your initial research.

The horse world has some interesting characters in it, so if you have one negative review and several positive reviews it's probably worth keeping that person on your list. On the other hand, if a trainer has mostly negative reviews, cross that person off your list. One or two bad reviews out of many good ones might not mean much, but more negative than positive is a big red flag.

Always listen to your gut when you are meeting someone. If the trainer sets off warning bells in your head, find someone else to work with.

There will be some areas of the country where pros in a specific discipline are hard to find. Traveling to take lessons from a good trainer once or twice a month is better than taking lessons from a bad trainer eight times a month. To quote George Morris, the former coach of the United States

Equestrian show jumping team, "Perfect practice makes perfect."

Once you have done your research, you'll probably have a few options left on your list. Narrowing it down from here comes down to what the trainers have available and if you think you'll learn from their teaching style.

To get you started, here is a basic list of questions you can ask to help you determine who is right for you:

1. Are you available for lessons?
2. How much do you charge for lessons?
3. Do you offer group or private lessons?
4. Do you have lesson horses available?
5. How often do you and your students go to horse shows?
6. What type of horse shows do you attend? (local, regional, national)
7. How well do your students do at these shows?
8. What requirements do you have of your students?

If the answer to all of the above is satisfactory, it's time to go watch a few lessons. Do not show up at random. Make an appointment with the pro and go watch a few lessons to get a feel for his/her teaching style.

Take note of a few things while you watch the

lesson. Did the lesson start and end on time? What was the pro's teaching style? Do you think you are a good fit with that style? Did the instructor address any questions the student had? Was the student expected to tack up and warm up by themselves? If so, are you comfortable grooming, tacking and warming up a horse yourself? If not, does the pro or any of her assistants provide training to learn how to groom and tack up a horse?

The trainer will also ask you questions. Good trainers have limited time and often interview perspective clients to see if they will fit into their training system. Don't be surprised if you get asked a lot of questions. Just be honest about your goals and your skill level.

After you consider these questions, contact the trainer that fits your personality and budget the best and set up a time for a lesson. Don't forget to thank the other trainers for taking the time to talk to you.

If you are new to horses, I recommend taking lessons for at least six months before you purchase a horse of your own. This will give you time to learn the basics of riding and learn more about your own preferences when it comes to horses.

A First Horse Buying Experience

The first horse my non-horsey family ever bought came from an ad in the newspaper (which actually used to advertise quite a few horses before my town became a city). I scoured and scoured and finally called on a 5 year old POA (pony of the Americas) mare, safe for kids.

I was 11 or 12, with a week's worth of riding lessons under my belt, and it didn't occur to me that the phone number on the ad was a frequent flyer in the Horse Classifieds, but whatever. My parents drove me out to see this mare, who lived in an absolute dump (fences made of junk, horse trader living in a decrepit trailer house, loose animals and numerous unkempt horses everywhere, etc.).

The mare, a cute strawberry roan, was tacked up when we arrived (red flag which of course we did not recognize) and I rode her without incident. I'm sure I was in tennis shoes and no helmet because we were idiots and this was the '80s.

I remember thinking how odd it was that I couldn't get this nice young mare to trot or even jog under saddle.

So we paid our few hundred dollars and they delivered her (in a STOCK TRUCK, to a house full of noobs in the suburbs which obviously was not going to have a convenient earthen stock ramp).

You know what happens next. The drugs wore off and it turned out she was an unbroken 3 year old who liked to rear. She was never even safe to lead. She would blow and start rearing with no provocation, and we were utterly unequipped to handle behavioral issues like that or even know enough to call a vet to see if the behavior had a physical cause. We sent her away to the horse sale before I was seriously injured.

My parents invested in riding lessons on school horses after that, which was a much better choice for a lot of reasons.

Serena, Washington State

CHAPTER 3
DETERMING YOUR BUDGET

Nobody likes to talk about this part, but money is the number one determining factor for what horses you will look at. After all, there is no point in wasting your time or the seller's time if you have $10,000 to spend and they are asking $75,000 for their horse. You may reasonably expect to negotiate a horse's price down a small amount, but negotiating a horse's price down more than 10% would be a stretch.

While you may be thinking I have X amount of money to spend on a horse understand that a good horse purchasing budget covers more than just the price of the horse. There are transportation costs, prepurchase exam costs, and commissions to be paid in most horse purchase transactions. Let's look at the money it takes to get your equine soul mate into your barn.

Transportation Costs

Your horse search will require transportation for both you and your new horse. In some areas, horses are scarce, or perhaps horses that specialize in specific disciplines are scarce. If that's the case, you may have to do some traveling to find your perfect equine partner. Talk to your equine pro about what to expect as far as travelling. Are there a lot of horses available close to you? If so, you may just need to budget for gas. If not, you may need to budget for gas, hotels, meals, or even air fare.

Eventually, on one of these trips, you are going to find a horse that fits all of your criteria and you are going to want to bring him home. If you don't have a truck and trailer, you will need to hire a professional hauler. There are a lot of good haulers out there who will take great care of your horse and bring him right to your doorstep, but they do not provide this service for free. Most commercial haulers charge $2-$4 per mile and may have minimum rates. Be sure to budget at least a few hundred dollars to cover the cost of getting your horse home.

Pre Purchase Exam

Before you buy your horse, it is advisable to have a prepurchase exam done by a qualified veterinarian. Prepurchase exams can reveal physical problems before they pop up. This can keep your dream horse from turning into a lame duck two months after you buy him.

A prepurchase exam can be as basic or as in depth as you would like it to be, but the more in depth, the more expensive. A good prepurchase exam with basic x-rays and flexion tests can run $1,000-$2,000 and up. Don't forget to work this cost into your horse purchase budget.

Equine Pro Fees

Your equine pro is your best tool in finding your equine soul mate. Your pro knows your personality and riding abilities. A good pro will know the horse market, and have contacts to find horses for sale - sometimes before they even come on the market. Their advice can save you a lot of wasted time and frustration in your horse search.

They will also be well versed in equine conformation and can look for flaws that may affect how the horse would perform in your chosen discipline.

That said, they don't work for free. Talk to your pro about what they charge and what it covers. Some pros will do a percentage of the horse's purchase price plus travel expenses, and some work by an hourly fee. Whichever one applies to your situation, be sure to include it in your horse purchase budget.

Board

If you are planning on boarding your horse, you may have to pay to hold a stall at the facility of your choice. Some barns have waiting lists and will not hold a stall for you unless you pay a monthly fee to hold the stall. In many cases, you will want to board at the farm where your trainer teaches, but sometimes this isn't an option. Be sure to research where you will keep your horse before you start your search.

Board prices vary greatly and are largely dependent on your geographical region. In some areas, board at a very nice barn will cost $350 per month; in other areas, board at a very nice barn might cost $3000 per month.

Your purchase budget should include at least the first month's board, but many barns will ask for first and last month's board up front. Finding a place to keep your horse before you start shopping will help you budget the correct amount of money and give you peace of mind your new horse will have a good place to stay.

Insurance

Depending on the purchase price of your horse, it's a good idea to get insurance on your horse.

There are different types of insurance you can consider: major medical, loss of use, and mortality insurance.

Major medical insurance is similar to your health insurance. You pay a monthly premium and the policy will cover your vet bills after you pay your deductible. This insurance is important for any horse, no matter the value of your horse. Colic surgery costs the same on a $1,000 horse as on a $100,000 horse. If your horse has to spend time in a vet hospital for any reason, bills add up quickly. Most veterinary hospitals will run $500 to $1000 per day depending on location and treatment. Major medical can give you peace of mind that an injury won't drain your bank account.

Mortality insurance is similar to your life insurance. You pay a monthly premium and in the event of your horse's death, you are paid the value of the horse. Some insurers require a soundness exam or health certificate from your veterinarian or the veterinarian doing the prepurchase exam.

Loss of use insurance is an insurance policy you can have added onto your mortality insurance that will insure you if your horse becomes unable to do the job you purchased him for. For example, if you bought your horse to compete in the junior jumpers, and a pasture accident leaves him able to be ridden but not jumped, your loss of use policy would pay you a portion of the value of your horse.

Mortality and loss of use policies are usually recommended for horses with a purchase price over $10,000. If your horse costs that much or more, you should check into how much these policies will cost and figure the initial fees into your purchase price.

Purchase Price

Now that you have determined the budget for the all of the things associated with purchasing a horse, you can determine the purchase price. For most people, this becomes a simple subtraction problem. You had X saved for the purchase of a horse, subtract Y (the additional costs associated with purchasing a horse) and you get Z, the money you have to spend on the purchase price of the horse.

Prices of horses can vary greatly and for many reasons including age, training, ability, temperament, and breeding. The price of horses can also vary in different geographical regions. A rock bottom price for a basic trail horse could start at $1,500 in your area or they could start at $5,000. Ask your pro what you can expect to pay in your area, or if you will save money by traveling elsewhere.

In most cases, the more expensive the horse, the more training or ability the horse is likely to have. If you are just starting out, you do not need a horse that can run the fastest barrels or jump the highest fence. At your level, you are looking for a horse with good movement for your discipline and a horse with a good mind. Even if you don't have six figures to spend on a horse, you can still find a horse that will be a great partner for you.

CHAPTER 4
WHAT DO YOU WANT IN A HORSE?

Now that you know what discipline you are interested in, have connected with a good equine pro, and figured out how much you have to spend on your new horse, it's time to figure out what qualities you're looking for in your equine soul mate. There are many things to consider when narrowing down your search. Things like age, temperament, and breed may all play a part in finding the horse you are looking for.

You are looking for a perfect combination that fits your personality and skill level while staying on budget. The next section will walk you through just how to determine what you can and can't live without.

Determine Your Goals

What would you like to accomplish with your horse in the next one to five years? If you are an eventer and would like to show at the preliminary level in the next year, buying a prospect that has just started cross rails would greatly limit your ability to achieve your goals. If, on the other hand, you are a new rider who would like to do a few shows a year or two down the road, a horse that has a great mind, but not the ability to jump higher, might be just the ticket for you.

Spend some time thinking about what shows you would like to do, or trail rides you would like to go on. Ask your trainer for a little bit of advice on where she sees you in one to five years. Some people want to be at a very high level in five years, and some people are perfectly happy staying at the lower levels. Figuring out what you want your horse to do will give you a good starting point in finding the right horse for you.

Breed

Unless you plan on showing in breed shows, the breed of your horse will come down to the discipline you are riding in and preference. At the lowest levels, many horses can compete in many disciplines and be competitive. As you move up the levels in your discipline, breed may become more important, but at the lower levels brains take precedents over breed.

Certain breeds are bred to do a specific job and they are usually very good at it. Small, compact

Quarter Horses excel in reining and cow events. Big bodied warmbloods are bred to have the movement and spring to excel at dressage and jumping. A Tennessee Walking Horse has a smooth gait and plenty of stamina so you can trail ride all day.

Can a Tennessee Walking Horse jump? Yes, it can. Will it excel at it? No, probably not. Can a warmblood go out on trails all day? Yes, it can. Will you be sore at the end of the day from riding a horse with big, springy gaits? Yes, you might very well be.

Breed should not be the number one factor in deciding what horse is right for you. Try to stick to horses that have the body type or movement your discipline requires. As the old saying goes, "you can't ride papers."

Age

Unless you have a very good reason, the horse you buy should at least be old enough to be broke. For most horses, this would be around three years old. Horses and dogs have very little in common, so while you might get a puppy for the experience of training it or growing with it, doing the same thing with a horse is ill advised.

I say this for two reasons. First, if you buy a foal, you won't be able to ride it for a few years. In those few years, the horse can hurt itself and become unable to be used for your intended purpose.

Second, horses are big animals and without proper handling and training at a young age, they can become dangerous. Sticking to horses that are already broke will increase your odds of finding a horse you can accomplish all of your goals on and fall in love with.

Between the ages of five and 15 , the horse's temperament and experience level will be a more important factor in finding the right horse for you. Younger horses without a lot of training are generally less expensive than older horses with more training and a proven track record. Horses over 15 will start to lose their value a little bit as their age might limit their abilities.

Like humans, horses start to get a little wear and tear on them as they age, so a horse older than 15 may come with some joint stiffness that requires a supplement or monthly joint injections to keep him sound. If you are beginner rider, a 17-year-old school master might be your perfect horse. Talk to your trainer about maintenance and management plans, and you should be fine with a slightly older horse.

The Dead Quiet Horse

We went to look at a horse once that may or may not have been dead.

We were shopping for somebody's first horse and responded to an ad that sounded promising. We had no time due to a new baby, and we needed a teenage horse safe for beginners. Nothing super fancy, just something cheap.

We got to the farm and a family who looked like they had just finished seeing the horse were walking back to their car. They did not speak but made all sorts of crazy eye motions and subtle hand motions that couldn't be seen from the house behind them. They seemed to be saying, "You don't want this horse." No matter, we'd come this far.

We knocked on the door and the owner was too busy with three kids under five to show us the horse. But, they pointed in the horse's direction and said we should go try him. The owner not wanting to supervise strangers riding her horse was odd. No matter, we'd come this far.

He was standing alone in a field fully tacked up. Also very odd, but we'd come this far . We looked him over. He was probably older than advertised, but did seem beginner safe in that he didn't twitch or move no matter what we did.

The horse stood very still as our designated test rider mounts. He also stood very still as the rider clicked and squeezed his leg on the horses sides. He was still completely motionless as the rider gave a moderate tap with his legs, and again when we broke a tree branch and gave it to the rider an improvised crop.

A very solid kick on his side from the rider finally got a reaction from the horse. It was not the forward motion we had hoped for. It was a surprised grunt, so we suspected the animal was not actually dead, but who knows what sound a horse cadaver makes when you squeeze its rib cage hard.

We thanked the owner for her time and headed down the driveway. Going past another group of buyers on their way in, we made all sorts of crazy eye motions and subtle hand motions that would not be seen from the house behind us, trying to say, "you don't want this horse".

Luke, Maryland

Temperament

Like people, each horse will have his own temperament or personality. Some may be bolder than others, some more laid back. Some may be a little nervous and others could care less if a bomb went off next to them. What type of temperament are you looking for in a horse?

Your skill level is the first thing you should consider when thinking about temperament. If you are brand new to horses, a nervous or energetic horse won't be the best match for you at this stage. On the other hand, if you are an experienced rider, a horse with a little extra energy might be a good fit for you.

If you are new to horses and riding, you want to look for a horse that is tolerant of beginners. Some horses have never been ridden by beginners, so if you are new to horses, be sure to ask the owner if any beginners have ridden the horse in the past and how the horse handled it.

The other thing you should consider is your own personality. Are you the type of person who enjoys thrills or are you more laid back and relaxed? Are you competitive or shy? Thinking about the traits in your own personality can help you find a horse that fits you.

Someone who is very laid back may become frustrated with a horse that is high energy and spooky. Someone who is a big thrill seeker may become bored with a horse that is lazy and not in a big hurry to go anywhere.

The biggest thing you will want is a horse is a horse you feel comfortable riding, both physically and mentally. Even experienced riders can become frustrated or fearful of a horse they are not comfortable with, so if you are uneasy with a horse, it's wise to keep looking.

Ability

Ability alone will not make a perfect partner, but if you are planning on jumping 3'6 and the horse you purchase only has the ability to jump 2', you will have a big problem in a short time. You want to know the horse has the ability to get you to the level you want to go.

If the horse you are looking at has not performed

to the level you want to go to yet, it will take an experienced set of eyes to tell if the horse has the ability. It will also take training. Training takes time and money. If you buy a horse that isn't at the level you would like to be at, do you have the money to put the horse in training? Are you patient enough to wait while the horse gets to that level?

Keep these things in mind if you are looking at a horse that is considered a prospect more than a finished product. If you are an experienced rider looking for a horse to train up through the levels , the horse's ability to perform will have more weight than the experience the horse already has. On the other hand, if you are looking for a horse to show in the next year, the experience the horse already has should be given more weight than its future abilities.

Experience

Experience is how you know the horse actually has the ability to do what the current owners claim it can do. It's also a huge factor in pricing. A horse that has won a class at the national level will cost much more than a horse that has won a class at the local level.

If you are looking for a horse to barrel race, you will be able to review past times to see if the horse is performing at or near the level you would like to perform. If you are looking for a dressage horse, past scores will tell you how the horse has been performing and at which level.

Beginners or people looking to show the horse in the next year should be looking at horses that are currently showing at the level they would like to show at, or slightly above that level. This level of experience tells you the horse has the training and ability to do what you will be asking it to do and will give you a little leeway to make up for a beginner rider's mistakes.

Since horse buying is a buyer beware industry, you may want to contact the association the horse has shown at in the past. In most associations, you can look up a horse's past performances and some associations will show how many other riders were in the class. The number of riders can be an indicator of how well the horse you are looking at will perform in comparison to other horses.

For example, if a seller is advertising a horse that placed second at a big name venue, and you look and see there were only two horses in the class that day, it takes away from the credibility of the horse and the seller. Second out of two does nothing to speak to the quality of the horse, its performance on that day, or how well it will do when competing against other horses.

The Things That Don't Matter

I once had a client tell me she was looking for a

grey warmblood mare to do the jumpers on. We searched across multiple states, scoured the internet, and pestered all of my contacts. After three prepurchase exams that revealed major flaws, she finally relented and expanded her search. She ended up with a bay Thoroughbred gelding who was purchased an hour away from home through one of my contacts. He turned out to be the perfect horse for her and she has been very successful with him. The moral of this story is color should not be a factor in your horse search and, in most cases, neither should sex.

Most people have a color they think is beautiful (mine happens to be chestnuts). Maybe you love a grey horse like the client I mentioned. However, limiting yourself to one particular color will narrow your pool of choices to the point it may be impossible to find the perfect horse for you. Conformation, attitude, and ability should bear much more weight than the color of the horse.

The same thing applies to the sex of the horse. Mares and geldings are equally competitive across all disciplines and all levels so there is no reason to limit yourself to mares or geldings only. There are old wives' tales about moody mares and steady geldings, but they are just old wives' tales and should be taken with a grain of salt.

The one caveat to this is stallions. Although stallions can be wonderful sport horses, they require experienced handlers and many boarding barns will not accept a stallion. Sticking to mares and geldings will give you the most options and the best experience.

A Little Miscommunication Between Seller and Buyer

I answered an ad for an "aged gelding" while looking for a horse for my husband to event at the lower levels.

I called first to speak to the seller and told her what we wanted: an older horse suitable for a novice rider and capable of eventing. The seller thought it could work, and I made an appointment to see the horse.

I make the drive and found the horse in pasture. The owner shows me how he lets her approach, tells me how kind he is, blahblahblah. The horse seems serviceably sound and has a nice enough personality so I make a second appointment to let my husband come out and give the horse a test ride.

We arrive at the farm, the owner tacks up the horse for us, and my husband tries him out in an outdoor arena. He looks stiff and my husband says he feels stiff. After about 10 minutes of walk and trot, the horse does not seem to be working out of it. Whereupon owner totes out a LARGE container of various supplements and meds horse is on.

I ask if all of this keeps him sound enough to jump at most 3' - she is aghast & tells me he can't be jumped, E-V-E-R.

So, what part of "event" did she not understand on the initial call or 1st visit?

Anonymous

CHAPTER 5
HORSE SHOPPING

Finally, the part you have been waiting for: horse shopping! You have a little experience and you know what you are looking for, and now it's time to go shopping. Horse shopping will be one of the most exciting and most frustrating things you may ever do.

Some horses will not be as advertised, some will check all the boxes on your list but not feel quite right, and eventually you will find your equine soul mate. The most important thing when looking for a horse is to let your heart lead you but let your head make the final decision. If a horse doesn't seem quite right for any reason, don't purchase it. You and the horse will be happier in the long run.

Keeping Track

The process of horse shopping can be long and you will probably look at several horses. It's a good idea to keep track of the horses you are looking at. A notebook or Excel spreadsheet with names, phone numbers, and notes about the horse will help you keep track of the horses and narrow down your list.

It will also come in handy if you are paying your equine pro by the hour. You can use your notebook or spreadsheet to keep track of when your pro came with you, how long the process took, and how much money you will owe her at the end of the day.

The Great Horse Search

All of this happened during one horse search.

First, it was a grey that had upper level eventer blood.

We went to see her and she had a huge deep crack in her hoof that left the poor mare crippled. The owner didn't see a problem and said, "All the horses are like that."

At the next farm were two horses I went to see.

Preston was a dark bay with chrome and BEAUTIFUL. He was out of our range but my mother said "ok," and we tried him out. I took him to the arena (with no fence and some ice) and the owner said I could get on and he would be fine. I was 12. Preston was pretty good... until he wasn't. He ran through the bit and took off with me. It's a good thing I was a decent rider and got him under control. Our ride was basically over.

Then, the owner pulled out this homely Trakehner at 17.1 hands. I LOVED HIM. All was well and we set up another time to come try him out. We showed up and owner was nowhere to be found. She wouldn't answer the phone. We just wandered around and found Mudslide in a back paddock and the barn owner said he was sold. It broke my heart and then the owner finally called back and tried to force Preston down our throats. We declined.

Another horse we looked at was at Frying Pan Auction for a reserve on the lower end. I rode the horse and he upped his price 3x after the ride (we were going to buy him before auction).

I went and rode a young newly gelded Thoroughbred. He was super cute and well behaved. Somehow, my mother started talking to the owner about our previous run in with the horse above named Preston. He knew the horse and the owner very well. I guess Preston was a hunter that got burnt out and turned into a hot uncontrollable spaz. The owner was a liar, no surprise. We figure Mudslide wasn't sold but she knew he wouldn't pass a PPE so she tried to off Preston on us.

We finally found the guy we purchased after looking at countless horses in West Virginia, Pennsylvania, Maryland, and Virginia. Wow, that was a learning curve for my 12-year-old self.

Kristi, Florida

Contacting the Seller

Depending on the setup you have with your equine pro, you may or may not be the person initiating the initial contact with the seller. Even if you are working with a pro, you can still do some searching on your own and, in those cases, you will be the one contacting the seller. When conducting your own search, stick to the criteria you came up with in the last section, do not let pretty pictures lead you astray.

If you find a horse you're interested in, follow the instructions on the ad to contact the seller. Some ads will request calls, some emails, and some will request you have your pro contact them.

In the initial contact, describe what you are looking for and what you plan on doing with the horse. Then, give the seller the opportunity to tell you if they think the horse will work for your purposes. The seller knows their horse the best, if they don't think the horse will be a good fit, it probably won't be.

If you both agree the horse might be a good fit, now is a good time to ask questions about the fitness of the horse, how much training the horse has, and why they are selling the horse. Listen carefully to the answers, make a few notes in your purchasing notebook, and then decide if the horse is worth pursuing further.

You should ask questions relevant to your

discipline, but here are a few general questions you can ask about a prospect.

1. **Has the horse ever been injured?** This question is good to ask for future reference. Many horses have been injured and heal up just fine, but if you do end up purchasing the horse, you may ask the vet to pay particular attention to the previously injured area.

2. **Is the horse shod and is his usually shod?** This question gives you an idea of how his feet are and if the owner is ready to show him. If he is not shod but usually is, his way of going will be affected by not having shoes on. If he usually isn't shod and is ridden regularly, this can speak to the quality of his feet.

3. **How does the horse act when taken off the property?** This question can give you some insight into his personality. Some horses are perfect angels at home and get very nervous when taken off the property. Some horses couldn't care less if they go someplace new. Asking this question will let you know which one your prospect falls into.

4. **Does the horse load onto trailers well?** Presumably you will not be able to walk this horse home, so his trailer loading skills will become

important very quickly.

5. **Does the horse stand for the farrier/baths/clipping?** Some horses will be fine for baths but need drugs to be clipped. It is good to know where this horse stands, or doesn't. A horse that does not stand for these things is not an automatic "no," but it does tell you a little bit about the horses personality.

6. **What is the horse's registered or show name?** Unregistered horses might have a name they're shown under, and even registered horses may have a different show name. Having this information will help you do your research on the horse's past performances.

7. **Where has the horse shown and what prizes has he won?** Once the seller gives you this information, you can check with the organizing body to make sure the seller is giving you accurate information.

8. **Confirm the price.** Sellers sometimes advertise horses in multiple places and may have different prices listed in different areas. Typos have also been known to happen, an extra zero can have a big effect on the price.

Remember, you do not have to decide if you would like to see the horse while you are on the phone with the seller, a simple "thanks I will get back to you" will work just fine. This will give you a chance to mull it over and get the opinion of your trainer.

Double Check the Price

My sister-in-law was shopping for a hunter prospect and our trainer found a young gelding with a sales price of $15,000. He was advertised on several Facebook groups, sales websites, and she knew his trainer personally. He moved and jumped well so my sister-in-law, trainer, and I drove down so she could try him.

The horse was amazing, and my sister-in-law was getting along really well with him. Our trainer starts asking how negotiable the price is and his trainer says she's firm at 150. My trainer and I look at each other confused and ask what she means....again, she says the price is firm at 150!

Apparently, there was a TYPO in all of the sales ads and the horse was $150,000, not $15,000! We had to break the news to my poor sister-in-law as she is happily riding around on what she thinks is going to be her new horse. Uh, sorry - he's a little out of your budget

Holly, Missouri

Setting up an Appointment

Setting up an appointment where everyone can attend can be frustrating. The best idea is to ask the seller for a few times that would be convenient for them, consult with anyone you plan on taking with you, and then call the seller back and make a concrete appointment.

If the horse you are looking at requires a long trip, ask the seller to notify you as soon as possible if a problem comes up. In the same light, no matter how far you're traveling, if you are running late or cannot make an appointment, be sure to let the seller know as soon as possible.

The most important part of setting up an appointment is clear communication. Besides knowing what time to be there, now is also time to ask any questions or make any special requests. If you would like to see the horse doing something particular, ask the seller to be prepared for your request. If you would like to ride in your own saddle, ask the seller if this will be an issue. If you would like to see the horse being caught from a field and tacked up, let the seller know. Clear communication will make the whole process go smoothly for everyone involved.

First Impressions

A prospective horse is new to you, always approach a new horse with caution. Even if you have seen a video of a cowboy standing on top of the horse firing a pistol, you don't know the horse's quirks. Proceed with caution.

Stand back and take the horse in. Look at the horse's conformation at all angles. Notice how the horse interacts with its current owner and pay attention to anything the current owner does differently than you would do it. Most of the time, this is simply a difference in practice. As the saying goes, there is more than on way to skin a cat. Still, asking about anything you find odd is perfectly acceptable.

First impressions can be misleading. You might walk up to the horse and think "no way," especially if you have only seen show pictures of the horse. This is kind of like only seeing pictures of your date in a tux, and when he knocks on your door to pick you up, he is wearing jeans and a t-shirt. The reverse can also be true. Some horse owners aren't great photographers so when you see the horse in person, as opposed to in videos or pictures, he can look much nicer than you expected.

No matter if your first impression is positive or negative, make a mental note of it, and move on with the showing. First impressions do not give you much information to go on, they're just quick visual impressions. The jeans and t-shirt guy might prove to be the most comfortable and fun horse you have ever ridden, and the stunning tuxedo horse might dump you on your head. Either way, give them a chance. There is a reason you went out to look at the horse!

Tacking up

Even though you are excited to interact with what could be your new horse, it's wise to stand back and let the current owner tack up the horse while you observe. This is a good time to ask about tack, saddle width, and any fitting problems the current owner has had in the past.

Ask about the bit the horse is currently using and any bits they have tried in the past. If the owner uses any other equipment besides a basic saddle and bridle, now is the time to ask about it. If there is a piece of equipment you are unfamiliar with, ask not only why they use it, but how that particular piece of equipment works.

As the horse is being tacked up, look for signs of discomfort in the horse. A horse with ears laid back, nipping and biting at people or himself is a sign of discomfort. While this alone may not be something to make you pass up the horse, it's a good idea to ask the current owner about the behavior. Is it new? Have they tried anything to curb the behavior or make the horse more comfortable?

The First Ride

Unless there is a very good reason, the owner or an agent of the owner should ride the horse first. This will give you and your trainer a chance to watch the horse move and notice any quirks the horse has. The owner should ride the horse at all gaits and do anything special your discipline requires (i.e. jumping, slides, barrel pattern). If there is something specific you would like to see the horse do, ask the owner.

The next step will either be for you or your equine pro to ride the horse. This generally depends on your ability level and your comfort with getting on strange horses. As a general rule, I usually ride the horse before I let a client on, but there are always a few exceptions. Discuss this with your trainer before you get to the farm.

If your trainer does ride first, pay attention to any differences the horse shows with your pro rather than the owner. Most horses will show subtle improvements with a professional on board. A horse that shows a huge improvement when ridden by your pro is a red flag. Horses of this nature know the ability of the person on their back and will only perform up to the rider's ability. This can be very frustrating for an amateur owner who is learning to ride.

Finally, it's your turn to ride. Your trainer will

guide you on what to do according to your skill level. Your job is to determine how comfortable you are with the horse. Do you feel balanced on the horse? Do you feel in control of the horse? Most importantly, are you having fun?

You should enjoy riding the horse. A horse that ticks all of your boxes but doesn't make you smile is not your equine soul mate. You are looking for a horse that ticks most of your boxes and you enjoy riding. Some days it might feel like you are looking for a unicorn, but the right horse for you is out there.

When to Stop A Showing

If at any time you feel in danger either from the horse or owner, stop the showing. If you feel like the horse may kill you, thank the owner for their time, hop in your car, and cross that horse off of your list. You do not have to complete a showing. Most owners will appreciate your honesty.

If it is the owner making you wary, you can just leave. You don't need to apologize, make up excuses, or anything else if you are truly afraid for your life. Just wave over your shoulder and head for your car. This is a good reason to bring someone along to view the horse. There is safety in numbers.

You can also stop the showing as soon as you are positive you won't be purchasing the horse. There is no reason to continue if you are sure this horse is not your dream horse. Again, thank the seller for their time and head off to see the next horse on your list.

Red flags

As I mentioned earlier, horse shopping is a buyer beware situation. There is not a lot of recourse if you purchase a horse that doesn't turn out to be quite what you planned it to be. Here are a few things I have seen in the past that sent the red flag flying.

- **Horses that are lame.** Sometimes, this really isn't the fault of the seller. The horse was fine yesterday only to walk out of the stall today with a major limp. No matter how impressive the horse is on paper, you cannot properly evaluate a lame horse. If the horse is amazingly nice, you can keep in contact with the seller and come back at a later date if the horse becomes sound again.
- **A horse that is sweating when you show up** (unless it is 100 degrees out). This often means the horse has been heavily worked before your arrival. A seller might do this to take the edge off of a horse with too much energy.
- **Excessive tripping or stumbling.** This can be a sign of a neurologic disorder or a horse that has been tranquilized. Either way, you don't want that

horse. Horses do occasionally trip or stumble, especially with an unfamiliar rider, but a horse that repeatedly trips or stumbles is one you should pass on.

• **The seller would like to bring the horse somewhere to meet you.** Sometimes there is a good reason for this, like the seller not having a proper arena or safe jumps. But, I would at least want to see the horse at home once, and then perhaps follow the seller over to another place where they have the required equipment.

• **A horse that is already tacked up when I get there.** In instances where I have had this happen, I ask the owner to untack the horse, and start over. An already tacked up horse can be an attempt to cover up behavior problems or a physical malady the owner doesn't want you to see at first glance.

• **Buyback or first right of refusal clauses in a contract.** A buy back clause says that if you decide to sell the horse for any reason, you will give the seller the option to purchase the horse back before offering to anyone else. The problem with these clauses is you have no way of predicting the future value of the horse. If the clause states something like, "Buyer will offer the seller the horse at a price to be determined by an equine appraiser agreed upon by both parties," I might consider it. Otherwise, my client or I has paid for the horse, and it is ours to do as we wish.

• **Refusal to sign a sales contract.** I saved the biggest red flag for last. A sales contract protects the buyer and the seller. Refusal to sign a contract for any reason is a huge red flag. No contract, no money changes hands!

This is a list of some of the major things that have made me cautious or outright pass on a horse in the past. It's not a complete list, and if something seems out of the ordinary, listen to the little voice in your head and proceed with caution.

Horse Thief!

I was horse shopping in the $20Kish price range for a green hunter and some ads appeared for several nice horses, all from very different backgrounds. I saw two that seemed to fit the bill but went to see other horses and the ads went down before I could call.

Then the ads popped up again, but with a different address (different state but still local), different barn name, different seller, and the seller had a bunch of horses for sale. All were different types of horses for sale, really random. From an Appaloosa/draft cross to papered imported warmbloods and everything in between.

I consulted Google and a couple had recently been bought for cheap at one of the Professional Auctions (back when they had one in NJ), but the others didn't seem to come from there. I figured the seller was a flipper but that alone isn't a no go for me, so I called to make an appointment.

We went there and it was this c-r-a-z-y place where you'd never expect a barn to be, it was basically on top of a mountain. I used the restroom in the house and they were clearly living out of boxes. Very bizarre. None of the photos in the ads had been taken by them because the setting and horses looked completely different. The horses were every range of condition, some were show ready and some you could count the ribs on.

None of the stories the "trainer" who showed me the horses made sense for any of the horses. She plain lied about the ones I had tracked from the auction.

I rode two and liked one. The ring was really small and you could barely fit one jump in there, but I jumped the horse I liked and she packed around.

I went back with my then trainer for a second ride the very next weekend and the horse was like a completely different horse. She stopped at a jump with my trainer (who was an eventer and doesn't have a problem getting a normal horse over a fence). She was just generally sour and difficult, completely different under saddle. So, we passed.

The "owner" (not the owner's trainer who had shown us the horse) called me a few days later and offered me the horse for $2000. It had been for sale for $20,000. I passed again.

About a week later, I was googling the horse again because

I was so curious about the whole situation and a local newspaper article came up about how several horses (including this one) were stolen and the police had arrested the "owner" and her boyfriend for the theft!

Veronica, New Jersey

CHAPTER 6
THE PURCHASE PROCESS

Once you decide on a horse, it's time to navigate the purchase process. Each transaction will be a little bit different but there are some general standards across all horse purchases.

Contracts

No matter who you are dealing with, get a sales contract. In your contract, be sure to include a description of the horse, any registrations or paperwork the horse has, the purchase price of the horse, how any deposits will be dealt with, and how the seller is to be paid. If you are using an equine pro, be sure to address how commissions will be paid and by whom (doubly important if the seller is also using a pro to help them get the horse sold).

Anything and everything you have agreed upon with the seller should be in the contract, including trial periods, prepurchase exams, and included tack. Everything.

The contract does not have to be something drawn up by a lawyer. It can be on a piece of notebook paper as long as it is signed by both parties and a witness, and both parties have a copy of it. The most important thing here is that all parties understand and agree, in writing, to everything that has been discussed.

Deposits

If you are seriously interested in purchasing a particular horse, you can put a deposit down to hold the horse. A deposit will keep the seller from selling the horse to another party before you have a chance to arrange a prepurchase exam. Most sellers will not hold a horse without a deposit; they have been burned too many times by people promising to set something up and then disappearing, never to be heard from again.

The amount of the deposit you need to leave is between you and the seller, but standard practice is a 10% deposit. If you think you will need longer than a week to set up the prepurchase exam and decide on the horse, a higher deposit is reasonable as the seller is taking a greater risk holding the horse for a longer period of time.

As soon as you reach this step, you should get a contract in place. Make sure you understand and agree to how much of your deposit is refundable should you decide against the horse for any reason.

Prepurchase exams

A good prepurchase exam is a something you should get done on any horse you are planning to purchase. There are some times when the owner doesn't even realize there is a problem. In the past, I have found heart arrhythmias, rotations in coffin bones, and in one case, an x-ray showed a hole in a hock joint.

Find a vet in the area who preferably has not seen the horse before and get an appointment set up. The vet will ask you what you intend to do with the horse and at what level. This will help the vet determine the suitability of the horse and what tests he believes need to be performed to get the answers you're looking for.

In general, lower level horses are given a more basic exam then upper level horses. Ask your pro what they feel is an appropriate level of testing for the horse you are looking at.

The one thing you should note about a prepurchase exam is they are not pass/fail tests. The vet is there to advise you on any issues he has found and tell you about the suitability of the horse for its intended purpose. He will not stamp "pass" on a piece of paper and send you on your way.

Consider this scenario: You are looking for a horse to do dressage up to first level. You are considering an older horse and in the prepurchase, the horse shows a little bit of arthritis and general joint stiffness. The vet tells you he thinks with some management, the horse can perform at the level you require.

If the vet were examining the same horse but the prospective buyer wanted the horse to jump four foot fences, the vet may tell the prospective buyer the horse will likely not hold up for that level of performance and concussion on his joints.

If you are confused about the vet's recommendations or have concerns about a finding in your prepurchase exam, ask questions and consult with your trainer or pro.

Trial period

Trial periods are becoming rarer and rarer these days, due to too many horror stories on the internet about horses that come back sick, lame, or worse, not at all. In some cases, trial periods are still granted for a week or two so you can see how you will do with the horse on your own.

If you are granted a trial period, there are a few things you will need to expect. First, you will either have to pay for the horse in full or fully insure the horse for the purchase price before the horse leaves the sellers property. You might have to do both. Second, there may be restrictions on what you can do with the horse during the trial period. Some sellers will restrict where you can keep the horse, what you can feed the horse, and so on. Make sure the trial period and any stipulations are written into your contract.

During the trial period, try to do the same things you would do with him if you owned him. Turnout, riding, and lessons should all be as close as possible to the situation you will keep the horse in. Some changes will have to wait until you actually purchase the horse, but keeping things as close to how you would have them will give you a much better trial of how the horse will interact in his new environment.

Payment

Unless you have arranged otherwise, payment is due in full before the horse leaves the seller's property. Most sellers will accept cash, a cashier's check, or a bank transfer. A few sellers may take credit cards, but don't count on it. If you need to delay payment for any reason, let the seller know beforehand and make sure it is written into your contract.

Buyer Beware!

*I reached out to a trainer about a dressage prospect. We communicated via email and established a time and date. I asked her to let me know if anything came up since the horse was quite nice and *very* reasonably priced.*

The morning of the appointment I reminded her that I was coming in from out of state. I arrived around lunch (solid eight hour drive).

She pulled the horse out of his stall and he was missing a massive chunk out of his hip and was literally dragging his back leg (thuthunk over the shavings board in the stall and everything.. She casually shrugged it off and said he must have gotten into something out in the pasture overnight. She never offered an apology for wasting my time, explanation for why she didn't warn me via text/call, or any real concern about the horse's welfare.

She then tried to show me several other horses all with some degree of lameness with an assortment of excuses (trimmed short, played too hard in the field, lazy). It was then I pieced together her source for these prospects appeared to be either a meat buyer or local auction as every horse had the same vague background and description of ability.

I carefully got myself out of the situation, said a prayer for that poor horse, and hit the road.

Taylor , USA

CHAPTER 7
BRINGING YOUR NEW HORSE HOME

The check is written and your new horse is on the trailer. Before you leave the seller's property, it is a good idea to get a little bit of information from the seller about how your new horse has been managed in the past. Remember, you bought this horse because he is awesome. The prior owner's management had a lot to do with that, so finding out how they managed the horse is always a good idea.

Feed

Hay should make up the majority of any horses diet. Check with the previous owner to see what type of hay the horse has been getting and if there have been any problems with hay in the past. Your new guy may be finicky or may be allergic to some hay.

Sudden changes in grain can cause colic and

attitude changes in horses, so it's a good idea to find out what type of grain and how much he has been eating. If you are planning on changing your horse to a different grain, make any diet changes slowly to avoid any stomach upset in your new horse.

To avoid major attitude changes, try to find a grain that is close to what he is already getting in fat and protein content. If you plan on riding the horse more or less than the previous owner, the horse may need a feed with a different fat and protein content. Start with minor changes in content and evaluate from there.

Turnout

Before bringing your horse home, you need to know what type of turnout the horse has been getting and for how long. A horse that has been turned out with mares and geldings for eight hours a day may not be happy in a private turnout situation. A horse that has been turned out 24/7 can show major attitude changes if he is suddenly kept in a stall for 16 hours a day.

There are times when it just isn't possible to manage the horse like the previous owner managed him. A large boarding barn may not have the capability or pasture available for a 24 hour turnout situation, or they may only offer private turnout.

Whatever the case, monitor your horse carefully for the first few weeks. If the horse goes from a 24 turnout situation to an eight hour turnout situation, he may have more energy than you would like, you may have to pay your pro to ride him each day. If he is used to being out in a group and he seems lethargic by himself, see if you can put him in a place where he has a different neighbor or is in view of more horses.

Most turnout situations can be managed. You just have to figure out what is best for your horse within the constraints of your facility.

Tack

Before your horse comes home, you should ask the seller about the tack the horse is usually ridden in. Some horses may go in different bits for different situations, require a martingale when jumping, or need a breast collar because of their narrow build. Ask a lot of questions to determine if they have tried other things, or if this is something all of their horses are ridden in.

You can ask the seller what type of saddle they use to give you a general idea if your current saddle will fit your new horse or if you will have to find some new tack to go with your new horse.

Most English saddles are measured as narrow, medium or wide trees. With Western saddles, you may hear the term "bars" instead of tree. Terms including "full quarter horse bars" and "half quarter horse bars" refer to the width of the saddle tree.

The width of the tree determines how the weight is spread across the horse's back and how much freedom of the shoulder a horse will have.

Just like jeans on humans, different saddles will fit horses differently even within the same size range. In some cases, you may be able to have a saddle fitter come out and fit your current saddle to your new horse instead of buying a new one. To find a saddle fitter in your area, contact the manufacturer of your saddle. Many saddle fitters only work with specific brands, and contacting the manufacturer will be the quickest way to find one who works on your saddle.

Ask about the bit they are using. You will want to know what bit the horse is currently using and if they have tried any other bits and the results. You will also want to know the size of the bit the horse uses. Bits are measured by the width of the piece that goes in the horse's mouth, and is usually measured in quarter inch increments. An ill-fitting bit can bang a horse' s teeth or rub the corners of his mouth and cause pain and discomfort.

CHAPTER 8
AUCTIONS AND FIRST TIME HORSE BUYERS

As you can see, buying a horse can be a lengthy process. Some buyers hear about the "deals" they can get at auction and want to go that route. I discourage auctions for purchasing your first horse. The truth is some people do get great deals at auctions, but the majority of people come home with a problem horse. The people who do get great deals also come home with problem horses, but they also have the experience to solve those problems and make the horse a good horse.

If you purchase a horse at auction, you are also missing a huge chunk of information about the horse. You might get to talk to the seller you might not. You might get to ride the horse first, or you might not. When the horse walks in the ring, all shined up to be sold, the only information you have is just how pretty he is. You don't know his

background, you don't know his training or show history, and you don't know how he has been managed.
Buying a horse from a private seller who can give you all of that information and more is a better way to spend your hard earned money. It also exponentially increases your chances of finding the perfect horse for you.

Many experienced horsemen and women will not purchase a horse at auction because they do not have the time, money, or desire to deal with the problems that come from auction horses. If you are new to this, take a page out of their book and stick to the private sellers.

Hard to Mount?

I bought a horse led through a sale that was said to "ride and drive, but be a little hard to mount." I bought the horse, and when I went to pick it up from the sellers, I asked how hard he was to mount. Their reply? "We don't know. We never did manage."

Esther, Maine

SOME FINAL THOUGHTS

Buying a horse is a process unlike any other. You are buying a living thing, often for large sums of money after only having seen the horse a few times at most. This process has been compared to car buying and house buying; it is really that big of a purchase. Purchasing a horse can put you on an emotional roller coaster the likes of you have never seen before.

Remember to lead with your heart but make decisions with your head. Do not let your heart talk you into buying a horse because you feel bad for it, or because it looks just like Black Beauty. Pity purchases rarely work out, and Black Beauty was a fictional character.

Listen to your equine pro; it's what you pay them for. They have years of experience and have seen countless horse and rider combinations and they have your best interest at heart. They are a little like your conscious, your mom, and your favorite professor all rolled into one. You pay them good money for their opinion - trust them to do their job well.

Having a trustworthy equine partner is a feeling like no other. You sit atop one thousand pounds of muscle and control him with a shift of your weight. This animal will carry you and your dreams around on his back. He will be your mane to cry on and a quiet place to think.

The relationship between horse and rider is a great one that many scholars have commented on over the years. If you are looking for your new equine partner, be patient. The right one will come along

ABOUT THE AUTHOR

Michele Cook has been involved with horses for most of her life.
Starting with 4-H when she was a child and moving up to the A levels
of horse showing. As an adult, Michele worked as a trainer and
riding instructor in the hunter and jumper industry for 15 years
before retiring as a trainer.
Currently Michele enjoys trail riding her two Tennessee Walking horses and works as a signalman for a Class 1 railroad She also writes along a blog all about simple ways to find your happiness. You can read more from Michele at
www.MichelesFindingHappiness.com